HORRIBLE JOBS IN

MEDIEVAL TIMES

Gareth Stevens
Publishing

**ROBYN
HARDYMAN**

Please visit our website, www.garethstevens.com.
For a free color catalog of all our high-quality books,
call toll free 1-800-542-2595 or fax 1-877-542-2596.

Library of Congress Cataloging-in-Publication Data

Hardyman, Robyn.
Horrible jobs in Medieval Times / by Robyn Hardyman.
  p. cm. — (History's most horrible jobs)
Includes index.
ISBN 978-1-4824-0339-8 (pbk.)
ISBN 978-1-4824-0342-8 (6-pack)
ISBN 978-1-4824-0337-4 (library binding)
1. Civilization, Medieval — Juvenile literature. 2. Middle Ages — Juvenile literature. 3.
Europe – Social conditions — To 1492 — Juvenile literature. 4. Europe — Social life and
customs — Juvenile literature. I. Hardyman, Robyn. II. Title.
D117.H37 2014
940.1—dc23

First Edition

Published in 2014 by
Gareth Stevens Publishing
111 East 14th Street, Suite 349
New York, NY 10003

© 2014 Gareth Stevens Publishing

Produced by Calcium, www.calciumcreative.co.uk
Designed by Simon Borrough
Edited by Sarah Eason and Rachel Blount

Cover Illustration by Jim Mitchell

Photo credits: Dreamstime: Armari36 20, Arquiplay77 13, Ginosphotos 25t,
Jeffthemongoose 9, Kalsers 36, Lorna 5, Maljalen 16, Mihalec 42, Nikonianart 34, Nopow
22, Razvanjp 7, Robo123 6, Rsooll 17t, Taiga 41, Vilant 40t; Shutterstock: Alb_photo 28m,
Anton_Ivanov 37, Natalia Bratslavsky 39, Chris2766 27, Ross Gordon Henry 11r, Joyart
10, Georgios Kollidas 4, Aleksei Makarov 40b, Maljalen 26, Lynea 19, 32r, Laurence
D. Matson 25b, Andreas Meyer 11l, Pakhnyushcha 32l, Panaspics 43l, Pio3 28t, 28b,
Aleksandrs Samuilovs 12, David Steele 45b, Sydeen 30t, Wansfordphoto 30b, Paul Wishart
29, Xpixel 33, Zerbor 21r; Wikimedia: 23, 45t, Georg Andreas Böckler 17b, The Bodleian
Library, Oxford 38, 43r, Limbourg brothers 8, 35, James le Palmer, The British Library 44,
Pepijntje 21l, Pethan 14,
Self 18, Simon Speed 31; www.aurorascarnival.co.uk: 24.

Printed in the United States of America.

CPSIA compliance information: Batch #CW14GS: For further information contact Gareth Stevens, New York, New York at 1-800-542-2595.

Contents

Chapter One
Medieval Times

The medieval period of history in Europe lasted roughly from the middle of the 1000s to 1500. In 1066, King William I of Normandy, in France, invaded England and defeated the king, Harold Godwinson, at the Battle of Hastings. He and his Norman knights took over the country, and the era of Norman rule in England began.

A Tough System

The Normans imposed a rigid system on society, called feudalism. This involved all levels of society, but, of course, the rich benefitted the most. At the head was the king. He gave land and castles to his barons, in return for their loyalty and service. Barons did the same for the next level down in rank, and so on. At the bottom of the heap were the peasants. They owned nothing, but worked for a lord. Feudalism was in place all over medieval Europe.

William the Conqueror reigned as king of England from 1066 until his death in 1087.

Religion

Christianity was an important part of everyday life in medieval times. Almost everyone went to church. They believed that God controlled every part of their lives. Even if their job was horrible and their life miserable, it was important to live a good life, in order to be rewarded after death.

Medieval churches, like this one, were built in every English village and town. Services were held through the week, with several on Sundays.

The King

Being king was the best job in medieval times. In England, there were several dynasties of kings over the period. The first five rulers were Normans, starting with William the Conqueror. In 1154, the Plantagenet dynasty took over. They had seven kings, through 1377. Finally, the royal houses of Lancaster and York ruled, through 1485. The next English dynasty was the Tudors, and with them began a whole new era.

Life in the Country

Most people lived in the countryside, in small villages. They worked very hard. Their homes were basic and not very comfortable. They often shared them with their animals. At least that helped to keep them warm.

Life in the country was hard work. There were lots of horrible and lowly jobs to be done.

The Cycle of the Year

Life was linked to the cycles of nature and the seasons. People started work at sunrise, and went to bed at sunset. It was often a struggle to feed a family, especially if the weather was bad and the crops failed. In a good year, any excess food was sold at the nearby market. The poor had very little money. They exchanged goods with each other, in a system called bartering.

Good Times

On religious festivals and holy days, people could rest from their work and have some fun. After attending church, there might be entertainments on the village green, with dancing and music for everyone. Jugglers, actors, and jesters performed for all. Children played games, such as soccer with an inflated pig's bladder.

The Miller

The miller was an important person in the village, but not a very popular one. He ran the lord's mill, which ground the grain to make flour. Everyone in the village relied on him to grind their grain, so he could demand high fees for the work.

Bands of musicians played for the villagers on holy days and other special days of the year.

Poor Peasant

Most people who lived in the countryside were peasants, called villeins. They were the poorest in society, and their life was incredibly hard.

The Lord Rules

Villeins had to work on the lord's land before they could farm their own small plots. It was backbreaking work. They were outside in every kind of weather. They plowed, sowed, and harvested his crops. They mended fences, dug ditches, and removed stones from his fields. This took 3 to 5 days a week. That left villeins little time to grow their own crops, which they needed to feed themselves and their families. And just when it was time to harvest their own crops, they had to harvest the lord's fields!

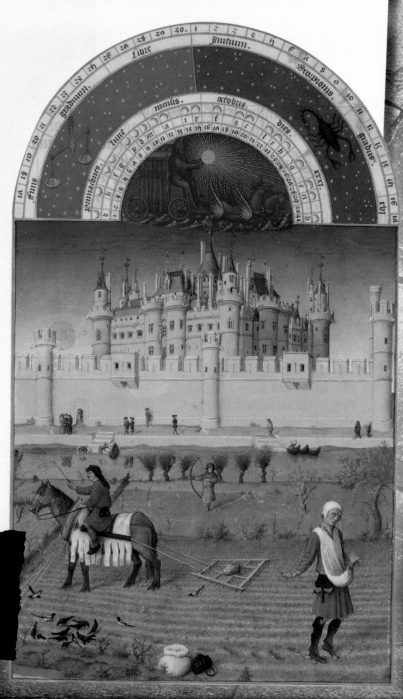

In fall, the peasants prepared the ground and sowed crops on the lord's land before they sowed their own.

A Woman's Work

Women did farm work every day. They fed the animals and grew vegetables in the garden. On top of their housework, they baked bread and even brewed beer, which people drank instead of water. They spun thread and wove cloth to make clothes. Women had very little say in their lives—they even had to ask the lord's permission if their daughters wanted to get married.

THE HORRIBLE TRUTH

Between 1315 and 1317, a great famine hit Europe and England. Heavy rains in spring and summer caused crops to fail, so people and animals had no food. Food prices soared, and millions of people died. On August 10, 1315, King Edward II of England stopped at the town of St. Albans on a journey. The famine was so bad that not a scrap of bread could be found to feed even the king himself.

Villeins also had to give a tithe to the church. This equaled one-tenth of their crops. Tithes were collected in barns like this one.

Deadly Wool Sorting

Most people's clothes in medieval times were made from wool or linen. Wool for weaving was spun from the fleeces of sheep. However, first it had to be sorted, and this could be deadly work.

A Fatal Breath

Spinning wool and weaving cloth were mostly done at home, by women and children. Piles of raw wool fleeces had to be sorted. They would be full of bugs, or even deadlier contents. Some sheep were infected with a deadly bacteria called anthrax. They caught it from the plants they ate. The tiny spores of this bacteria clung to sheep wool. As the children handled the wool, they breathed in the spores and became infected with anthrax.

Fields were full of sheep grazing. Sheep were kept both for their wool and for their meat.

Sheep were sheared for their wool fleeces, but these could contain the deadly anthrax bacteria.

Wool was spun into yarn, and made into clothes and cloth.

An Agonizing End

As the anthrax took hold, infected people began to sweat, cough, and ache all over. After a few days, their lungs collapsed and they fought for breath. They eventually died. This awful affliction was even known as woolsorter's disease, because so many wool workers got it.

Wool Wealth

Much of the wealth of the medieval period came from the wool trade. As spinning and weaving became more specialized, more and more of these tasks were carried out in town workshops by expert craftsmen. The buying and selling of raw wool and woolen cloth became big business.

Beastly Bog Iron

Many villages had a blacksmith. In his forge he made tools, hinges, and essential household objects out of iron. However, it was someone else's horrible job to find the iron itself.

Bogged Down

Bog iron is found in bogs or swamps. The iron in the water gradually forms lumps that collect in the mud and grasses. It was the job of a bog iron collector to wade out into the swamp to collect the iron. The water was freezing cold. Using a metal spike, the iron collector prodded the mud and grass for hours on end, hoping to hear the clunk of metal on metal as he hit a piece of iron ore. He then plunged into the mud, grabbed the iron ore, and put it in a basket, which got heavier as the day went on.

A bog iron collector spent all day wading through stinking, wet bogs in the search for precious bog iron.

Iron Wares

Without a poor bog iron collector, medieval people would not have had many essential items. These included tools for farming, pots for cooking, knives, weapons, and armor.

A blacksmith heated iron over an extremely hot fire, before molding it into shape.

A Wretched Job

The bog iron collector was probably a servant, or even a slave, who worked for the blacksmith. To shape iron, a blacksmith made a blazing hot fire, using charcoal, and heated the iron until it was red-hot. Then he hammered it, to make it stronger, before molding it into shape.

A Life of Woad

In medieval times, indigo dye was made from a plant called woad, and making it was a woeful way to earn a living. Woad plants were grown all over Europe, because the blue dye made from them was prized.

It was from the leaves of the woad plant that the dyers made their indigo dye.

Making Woad

First, the woad dyer harvested the leaves, chopped them into a paste, rolled them into balls, and left them to dry out for around a month. The next part of the job was the worst, because it smelled so bad!

Filthy Fermenting

Next, the woad dyer added water to the dry balls and they started to ferment with a powerful stench. Then the woad dyer added stale urine. This, as you can imagine, made the stink worse. The mixture was left for 3 days. Then, thread or cloth was dipped in it to dye the material. A woad dyer's hands and fingernails were permanently blue, and no one went near them!

Magic Transformation

When wool was put into the mixture, it didn't turn blue. That happened, as if by magic, the minute the wool was lifted out of the mixture and exposed to air.

Woad dyeing was a smelly job. The dyers could never get their hands clean!

15

Foul Fulling

Another part of the process of making woolen cloth was just as horrible. A fuller's life was also full of foul stinks.

Preparing Cloth

After woolen threads were woven together to make cloth, the fabric was coarse, with big gaps in the weave. The process of fulling closed up these gaps, making the cloth denser. It also washed away the natural grease left in the wool. The fuller's job was to trample the cloth in large vats of stale urine and water. Fullers collected urine from the locals, then trampled the cloth with their feet. The stink was overpowering, and it could take all day to work on just one batch of cloth. Fullers were fit, but very smelly.

Woolen cloth was woven by hand on looms like this one, although they were often much bigger.

Cloth woven on a hand loom was quite coarse in texture, and needed fulling to make it stronger.

No Mistakes

Fulling was skilled work. Cloth had to be trampled evenly, and the fullers had to know when to stop, or the finished cloth would be riddled with holes. When they had finished the job, fullers heaved the soggy cloth up onto a wooden frame and stretched it. The cloth was then left to dry in the open air. It was hard labor, but a respected profession.

Fulling mills, like this one, beat the woolen cloth with hammers. They were powered by waterwheels.

A Revolution

Fulling was one of the first processes to be mechanized. From the 1300s, it was often done in water mills. Waterwheels powered wooden hammers that beat the cloth. This was quicker, less exhausting, and much less unpleasant for the fullers.

Chapter Two
Life in Towns

Although most people lived in the countryside, towns grew bigger in medieval times. This was because they were centers of trade and crafts. Markets were held in towns, and houses were built around the markets. Town living conditions were mostly terrible, though, and there were plenty of horrible jobs to be done.

Escape to the Town

Towns offered a chance of escape for poor villeins. Every town had different rules, but, in some, if a villein managed to live there for a year and a day, he could become a freeman. Town life was tough, however. There was a lot of disease, and little food to eat.

Buildings such as this market hall were built around marketplaces. Gradually, the market towns grew in size.

Beggars

It was against the law for people to beg for money if they were fit and able to work. If a person was caught begging, they were put in wooden stocks for 3 days and 3 nights, as a public shaming. Their ankles or wrists were locked in place, and people threw rotten food at them. If the guilty person's shoes were removed, their feet were beaten, or tickled. Beggars were left in the stocks in all kinds of weather, and received only bread and water.

Beggars were often locked in stocks for days, and had rotten food thrown at them.

THE HORRIBLE TRUTH

Many beggars were lepers. They suffered from a horrible disease called leprosy, which infected the sufferers' skin and nerves. Eventually, pieces of their hands or feet rotted, and dropped off. Everyone kept well away from lepers, believing that they too would catch their vile disease.

Scary Stonework

Religion was at the center of medieval life. The most impressive signs of this are the many magnificent cathedrals and churches that were built in towns all over Europe. They are wonders of design, engineering, and art—but for the men building them, life could be very tough indeed.

Teamwork

Hundreds of different skills were needed to build a cathedral. Some men quarried the stone, others made the wooden scaffolding, laid roof tiles, or crafted the stained glass panels for the windows. A stonemason's apprentice had to do all the toughest jobs. The aim was to build upward, and to build high—the higher the better, because that meant the cathedral would be closer to God. Cities competed to build the tallest cathedrals.

Medieval stonemasons were highly skilled. With so much cathedral building, the best were in great demand.

A stonemason's assistant had to make sure tools were ready for when his master needed them.

This cathedral at Beauvais, in France, was the tallest building for miles around. The stone structures on the outside walls, called flying buttresses, supported the high walls inside.

Beauvais Cathedral, France

The cathedral builders in Beauvais, France, were determined to make the building the highest in the world. Work began in 1225, and the roof eventually reached an amazing, record-breaking 168 feet (48 m). However, a few years after it was finished, part of the roof fell down. It was soon rebuilt, but with more support. In 1573, an enormous central tower also collapsed.

A Master's Servant

Apprentices had to do whatever their master told them. They often had to work hundreds of feet up a building on unsteady wooden scaffolding to carve a block of stone or position a statue. They carried heavy materials and tools up and down ladders, and spent hours chipping away at blocks of stone.

21

Lousy Laundry

Most clothes were made of wool, and linen was used for underwear and household goods. All had to be washed, which in medieval times was a long, grueling, and smelly process. No wonder people didn't do it very often.

Bucking

It was the laundry worker's job to get the family's clothes clean. The best way to loosen the dirt and grease, and to get the whites white, was to soak the clothes in a mixture called lye, in a large tub. This was called bucking. Workers made the lye by mixing wood ash from fires with water. To get the whites really clean, stale urine worked even better than ash. Urine was collected from the household chamber pots. It made a great stain remover, but it sure did stink!

Ashes from fires were used to make lye for bucking. Different kinds of wood ash were used to remove different stains.

Most people could not afford soap. Wealthy people, however, had soap, although not as we know it. Medieval soap was made by mixing lye with boiled animal fat. Imagine washing with that!

Cold Wash

Laundry workers probably did all their work with cold water. Using fuel to make a fire to heat the water was too expensive. The bucking tub was an important household item. One is mentioned in the list of goods left by one of the Mayflower pilgrims, who died in 1633.

This painting shows servants bucking the laundry in tubs, hitting it to remove the dirt, and hanging the clean items out to dry. Their wealthy master could afford to heat the water over a fire.

Disgusting Gong Farmer

Gong farming may well have been the worst job in medieval times. Flushing toilets had not yet been invented, so it was the disgusting job of the gong farmer to get rid of everyone's poop.

Gong farmers were quite well paid, because their job was so awful.

Basic Facilities

Most people went to the bathroom in a pot in their house, and poured the waste down an open drain. In medieval towns, however, public toilets, called privies, were available. These were no more than wooden seats over a large hole, or cesspit, where the waste collected. It was a gong farmer's job to empty these cesspits. "Gong" means dung, or excrement. There was no pleasant, hands-off way to do this stinky job!

Nighttime Horror

Gong farmers worked only at night, and were sometimes known as "nightmen." Guided only by candle lamp, they scrabbled around in the cesspit, loading excrement into buckets. Just imagine the stink! Then, the buckets were hauled away, loaded onto carts, and driven out of town, where the stinking load was disposed of in an official dump. It was even sometimes used to fertilize the fields.

Gong farmers worked through the night, all year round.

THE HORRIBLE TRUTH

A castle toilet was called the garderobe. It was located at the top of a long chute on the outside of the building, so the waste fell down to the foot of the castle walls. If the chute became blocked, the gong farmer had to reach into the chute, or crawl inside, to clear the blockage. Yuck!

Gong farmers had to climb castle walls to clear garderobe chutes, if they became blocked with poop.

25

Chapter Three
Medieval Medicine

Medieval medicine was very basic, so becoming sick in medieval times was dangerous. As a result, life expectancy was short. Around half of all people died before they reached the age of 20.

Healing Herbs

If they were sick, most people went first to an apothecary. This was a person who dispensed drugs, which were made from herbs. Some of the drugs worked for minor ailments, up to a point. If people couldn't afford an apothecary, they went to the local "wise woman." She made up her own potions and medicines.

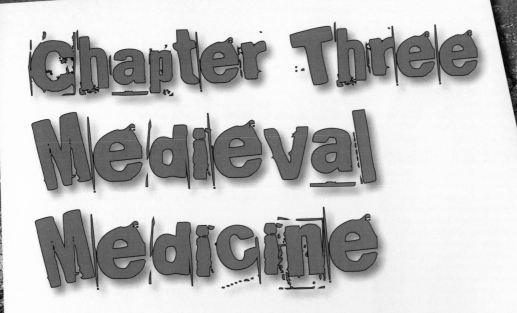

Apothecaries used books that described the properties of herbs and other plants.

Monks studied medicine at monasteries, such as this one in England.

Physicians for the Rich

Only the rich saw a physician. Physicians may have studied at a university and received some training in the basics of medicine. However, the basics were unlike the medicine we understand today. Medieval physcans believed that the body was made up of a balance between four substances called "humors." These were black bile, phlegm, blood, and yellow bile. Too much phlegm, for example, caused lung problems. Physicians looked for an imbalance in people's humors by examining their urine.

Religion and Medicine

Monasteries were centers of medical learning. Monks studied the properties of herbs and how to make medicines. Monasteries also developed the idea of hospitals. They started as hostels for travelers of all kinds, including those who needed medical help. They soon specialized as important centers of medical care, for both men and women.

Barber-Surgeon

The barber-surgeons were the most common type of doctor in medieval times. However, they were inferior to physicians, and their treatments were often pretty horrible.

Barber-surgeons used a selection of simple, but gruesome, tools.

Sickening Surgery

Barbers were licensed to use a blade. Their everyday job was shaving beards and cutting hair, but they could also put their blades to more gory uses. They charged high fees for surgery. Barber-surgeons made sure they got paid first—the patient didn't always survive to pay afterward! First, barber-surgeons diagnosed the problem by asking the patient to give them a sample of urine in a glass bottle. The barber-surgeon examined the urine, sniffed it, and swirled it around, looking for imbalances in the humors.

Terrible Treatment

The barber-surgeon might prescribe bloodletting, to cleanse the blood. The patient was cut and left to bleed into a bowl. If that didn't work, the barber-surgeon may have operated. There were no anesthetics to put the patient to sleep. Instead, the patient was tied down, firmly. The instruments used were probably quite blunt, and dirty, too. The poor patients were just as likely to die from an infected wound as from their original disease.

Guilds

People with a skilled trade, such as the stonemasons or barber-surgeons, joined together to form a group called a guild. These protected and controlled the practice of their trade in an area. They met together in a guildhall. The Barbers Company was formed in 1462. They joined with the surgeons in 1540 to become the Company of Barbers and Surgeons.

This house was built as a meeting place for the members of the wool merchants' guild in Suffolk, England.

Leech Collector

Would you like to spend all day outdoors and up to your thighs in cold water? If the answer is yes, then being a leech collector is just the horrible job for you!

Bloodletting

Bloodletting, to cleanse the blood, was an important part of the work of a barber-surgeon. This was sometimes done by cutting the patient, but another way was to use leeches. These long, slimy creatures love to drink human blood. They cling to the skin, pierce it, and take a good long drink. To find their blood-sucking leeches, barber-surgeons relied on leech collectors.

Leeches attach to a person's skin and suck the blood.

Marshy areas were perfect places for leech collectors to find leeches.

Wet and Cold

Leeches live in marshy areas. To catch leeches, bare-legged leech collectors waded out into the cold marshes, then waited. The leeches soon attached themselves to the collectors' legs. While the leeches feasted on their blood, the leech collectors picked them off and collected them in buckets. All the time, the collectors' wounds continued to bleed. Sometimes they would feel faint from the loss of blood. Germs in the water could infect their wounds and make them sick, too.

Jars like this one were used for storing leeches for medical use.

Leeches Linger

Believe it or not, leeches are still used in medicine today. Today, we no longer believe that bloodletting is helpful, but leeches are still applied to wounds after some kinds of surgery. Their spit contains a substance that stops the blood from clotting, or thickening. This can aid healing.

Putrid Plague Doctor

Probably the worst year ever to be a doctor in medieval Europe was 1348. This was the year that the plague, or Black Death, arrived from Asia.

Disgusting and Deadly

The Black Death was a truly horrible disease. First, painful black swellings grew on your body. When they burst, they oozed stinking pus all over you. Vomiting followed, and blood filled your lungs. Death came quickly, if you were lucky.

Plague was brought by rats on ships. Their deadly disease killed about one-third of the population of Europe.

It was easy to spot a plague doctor because their uniform was almost as scary as the Black Death itself!

All in a Day's Work

With this terrible disease wiping out entire towns and villages, plague doctors were in great demand, but there was little they could do. Treatments included rubbing the pus-covered body in butter and onions, or sprinkling it with dried, dead frog. And, of course, there was plenty of bloodletting. Eventually, the dead were loaded onto carts and taken away to be buried in mass graves.

Creepy Costume

Plague doctors wore a scary outfit. Their canvas cloak and leather pants were coated in wax, to keep out disease. Over their head went a dark leather hood, with a beaklike mask fixed tightly at the neck. Eyeholes were cut out of the mask and fitted with glass domes. All this was intended to keep the plague away. It certainly would have scared most people off!

Leeches sucked the blood of plague sufferers, but did not improve their chances of surviving.

Chapter Four
In the Castle

The castles of Europe are one of the wonders of medieval times. These magnificent buildings were fortresses, built to keep the lord and his people safe, and his enemies out. The rich had a comfortable life inside the castle, but the poor had plenty of horrible jobs to do.

So Many Servants

An army of servants looked after the lord, his family, and his estate. People slaved away in the kitchens, looked after the buildings, the horses and stables, and managed the lands owned by the lord. Personal attendants served the lord and his lady, answering all their needs. A band of soldiers was always on duty in the castle, to guard and defend it.

Bodiam Castle in Sussex, England, was built in 1385. It has four high towers at each corner, a massive gatehouse, and a moat for defense.

Warmth for a Few

In early medieval times, the great hall was heated by a huge fire in the center of the room. The room was a warm, smoky place where people gathered. Later, great halls were built with a large fireplace in one wall. The smoke went up the chimney. The lord kept warm by sitting closest to the fire.

The Hall

The great hall of the castle was the center of all activity. Everyone gathered there to eat, and most of the servants and soldiers slept there, too, on straw on the floor. Important meetings were held in the great hall, along with entertainments that included singers, dancers, musicians, and storytellers.

This French lord is surrounded by guests and servants at a lavish meal.

Deadly Crusader

Christian knights in Europe launched a series of expeditions to the Holy Land in the Middle East. They wanted to defeat the Muslims there, and take control of Jerusalem. These expeditions were called the Crusades, and for everyone involved they were often brutal and bloody.

A Holy War

The First Crusade was ordered by the pope and began in France and Italy in 1096. It took the crusaders 3 long and grueling years to reach Jerusalem. Many men died before they even arrived. Some were struck down by disease, which was common in the crusaders' camps. Others simply died of exhaustion from walking for endless miles each day. When the knights did finally reach their destination, they faced being hacked to death in battle by the fearsome Muslim armies.

The symbol of the crusaders was a red cross. Soldiers wore it on their clothing and armor. It was also used on army flags and banners.

Fight to the Death

In Jerusalem, the Seljuk Turks were in control. A terrible battle was fought, and knights received dreadful wounds. Eventually, there was victory. Jerusalem fell to the crusaders, and the Turks were driven out. About 100 years later, however, Saladin, the Muslim ruler of Egypt, recaptured Jerusalem from the Christians, and another gruesome crusade was launched. It failed, but many more bloody battles were fought over the next century.

Crusader Castles

After the First Crusade, most knights returned home, but some stayed to set up a kingdom in the Middle East. There, they built castles, such as the magnificent Krak des Chevaliers, in modern Syria.

Krak des Chevaliers was built for the crusading knights in the 1100s. It still stands today.

Scary Spitter

There were hundreds of hungry mouths to feed in the castle, and the kitchens were always busy. One of the sweatiest jobs was as a spitter. The spitter roasted meat over the kitchen's open fire. The roasted meat was later eaten by the castle's lord and lady, so the spitter had an important role.

Turning the spit to roast meat in front of the kitchen fire was hot, hard work.

Horrible Kitchen

The kitchen was located away from the main part of the building because of the risk of fire spreading. Across the front of the huge, open fireplace was an enormous spit. This was a long, metal rod on which meat was skewered. The meat was roasted in front of the fire for many hours. It had to be rotated, so that it cooked evenly. That was the horrible, sweaty job of the spit-boy!

Backbreaking and Hot

A spit could hold either several small pieces of meat—perhaps half a dozen chickens—or one huge animal. It was common to roast a whole pig. Turning the spit with the weight of a pig on it was backbreaking work. The spit-boys were almost as close to the heat as the pig! They sat in a small brick alcove, which stopped them from actually burning. The spit handle had to be turned slowly, for hour after hour. It could take all day to roast a pig or a sheep.

Mostly Meat

The rich ate a lot of meat, including beef, lamb, and pork. They also ate many types of bird, including pigeons, gulls, pheasants, geese, and even little quails and larks.

A whole roast pig could feed the many people who lived in the castle.

Endless Armorer

Knights needed armor to protect them in battle. There was plenty of fighting in the medieval period, so there was always lots of work for the armorer, whose job was to equip knights for battle.

It was easier for knights to move in flexible chain mail than in rigid plate armor. However, making chain mail took many hours of work.

Knights wore armor for protection in battle. The armorer crafted plate armor to fit a knight's body perfectly.

Chain Mail

At the start of the period, knights wore chain mail. This was made from thousands of metal rings, linked together to make a sheet of metal fabric. It was the dull, fiddly job of the armorer to make all those rings and join them together. Just one coat of mail contained 30,000 rings! A knight needed a coif, the mail covering for his head, plus a hauberk, the mail coat for his body. He also required hose, or leg coverings, so the armorers were always busy. In a battle, the mail could be badly damaged, so the armorer had plenty of repairs to do, too.

A Heavy Suit

A full set of chain mail weighed up to 30 pounds (13 kg). A full set of plate armor, however, weighed around 60 pounds (27 kg). Imagine trying to fight with that on your back!

Plate Armor

Chain mail was flexible, but it could be pierced by an arrow or sword. By the 1400s, most knights wore solid plate armor, which was heavier than chain mail and harder to make. Every suit of armor was tailor-made—it had to fit the knight exactly.

A suit of plate armor was a very expensive item for a knight to buy because it took so long to make.

Illuminating Monk

In medieval times, printing had not been invented. All books had to be written by hand. Most ordinary people could not read, but those who could wanted beautiful books to show off their wealth and status.

Learned Monks

Most books were written by monks. The lord in his castle would order a book and pay for the work to be done, either in his home or at the monastery. It was a long, tough job. Monks spent many hours, for months on end, carefully writing out each page. When daylight failed, they worked by candlelight, and their eyesight often suffered. In the monastery they worked in a special room, the scriptorium. It was cold and the monks suffered backache, numb feet, and cramps in their hands.

The skillful monks worked very long hours in poor conditions to create the beautifully decorated manuscripts we know today.

Books of Beasts

Not all books were religious texts. One popular kind was a bestiary, or collection of beasts. They described and illustrated many different kinds of animals and birds. Often, there was a moral lesson told with each illustration.

Bestiaries, such as this one, were very popular in France and in England in the 1100s.

Pen and Paper

The works of the monks are called illuminated manuscripts. This is because the words are "illuminated" with colorful drawn designs and illustrations. The inks had to be made by hand, and so did the paper. The best books were written on parchment, or vellum, which was made from lamb's hide, flattened and scraped smooth.

Monks had only candles to see what they were doing. It was a dark and lonely job.

A Changing World

The medieval period did not come to a sudden end, but during the 1300s and 1400s, life began to change for many people. There were still plenty of horrible jobs to do, of course.

A Better Life for Peasants

The Black Death killed so many peasants that the ones who survived could demand better conditions, and higher wages. Lords no longer needed them to make up their armies, because they now paid the king to hire professional soldiers for his army. The lord no longer needed to control the peasants and have them work his land. More of them became freemen. They paid cash rent to the lords, in return for living on their land or in their homes.

These plague victims are being blessed by a priest. Many people died of plague, so workers were in short supply. The survivors could demand better working and living conditions from their lords.

Printing

In the late 1400s, the printing press was invented in Europe, and many more books were made. More people began to learn to read. With greater education, it gradually became possible for some people to finally leave behind their horrible jobs.

With the invention of the printing press, more books were available for people to learn to read.

Castles and Towns

Kings also began to take back more lands from the lords, and became even more powerful. Castles became less necessary for defense, and more important as homes. The horrible jobs continued, of course, just as they did in towns. Gradually, more people moved to the towns, to trade and to develop skills.

Castles such as this one in Warwick, England, continued to dominate the landscape. However, they became more important as homes, and less important for defense.

Glossary

anesthetics substances that stop a patient feeling pain

anthrax bacteria found in wool fleeces that causes serious disease

apothecary a person who made medicines and potions, using herbs

apprentice a person who is taken on by a master to learn a new trade or skill

bartering exchanging goods and services without any money changing hands

bloodletting a medical treatment for cleansing the blood, by making the patient bleed

bog iron lumps of iron ore found in wet, marshy ground

bucking soaking laundry in a lye liquid to make it clean

buttresses structures built to support a wall

chain mail armor made from a metal fabric made up of thousands of joined rings

coif a chain mail covering for the head

Crusades "holy wars" fought by Christians against Muslims to win control of the Holy Land, Jerusalem

excrement human and animal waste

ferment to change chemically, after the addition of another substance

feudalism a system in society in which loyalty and service were given in return for land

fulling the process of washing woolen cloth to make it stronger and cleaner

garderobe a toilet in a castle

gong farmer a person whose job it was to remove human waste from cesspits

guild a union of workers with the same trade or skill, formed to protect the practice of that trade

hauberk a chain mail coat for the body

humors in medieval medicine, the four substances produced in the body, that had to be in balance for a person to be healthy

illuminated manuscripts pages of text and elaborate illustrations written by hand, usually by a monk

jesters medieval entertainers

leprosy a disease that infects the flesh and nerves of the body

life expectancy the average length of a person's life

lye a liquid mixture used for laundry

plague a highly infectious disease that killed millions of people in Europe in medieval times

privies toilets

spores the reproductive cells of bacteria

stocks a wooden framework with holes for a person's head, arms, or legs, used as a punishment

tithe a one-tenth share of a farmer's crop that was given to the church

villein a peasant farmer who worked a lord's land in return for a small piece of land to farm for himself

woad a plant used to make blue dye

For More Information

Books

Langley, Andrew. *Medieval Life*. New York, NY: DK Publishing, 2011.

Schlitz, Laura Amy, *Good Masters! Sweet Ladies!: Voices from a Medieval Village*. Cambridge, MA: Candlewick Press, 2007.

Steele, Philip, *The Medieval World*. Boston, MA: Kingfisher, 2006.

Websites

Discover all you need to know about medieval times on this great website. Explore the food, clothing, Crusades, music, and much more:
www.medieval-life-and-times.info/medieval-life/index.htm

Find out about knights, castles, and daily life in medieval times on this interesting and informative website:
www.ducksters.com/history/middle_ages_timeline.php

Check out this fun website to find out all about medieval Europe, from kings and palaces to knights and peasants:
www.kidspast.com/world-history/0195-mideval-europe.php

Index